Wellawatte Ways

A trek through the streets and homes of the people who lived in a small town called "Wellawatte", in the city of Colombo (00600), in old Ceylon (Sri Lanka) in the 60s

pic by Tharindu Amunugama May 2012

Fazli Sameer

To

The Wonderful People of Wellawatte

"Memories!
Wafting through the Windmills of our Minds"

Sameer, Fazli
Wellawatte Ways / Fazli Sameer,
Colombo 2021

ISBN 9798731018340

1.   People, Culture & Society, English

Wellawatte Ways
Fazli Sameer
Colombo, Sri Lanka
fazlis@gmail.com

First Print – 2021

ISBN: **9798731018340**

Published by: Fazli Sameer
Cover: Fazli Sameer
Printed by : Amazon/KDP

Foreword

This work started out sometime in the 2000s after the work on "Bamba" Days was nearing completion. The object of the exercise was to identify, map, and record, the streets, homes, and people, who lived around the streets, similar to what was done for the town of Bambalapitiya. The record begins at the Wellawatte Bridge and moves south all the way up to the Dehiwela Bridge at the famous "Williams" grinding mills junction.

Obtaining information by contacting those who lived in Wellawatte in the 60s was no mean task as many of them were off my radar.

Once I managed to put a reasonable amount of facts on to paper I then created an FB page titled, "I Love Wellawatte" and was able to receive many more responses and facts about the town.

This has now evolved into a huge canvas of the town of "Wella", remembered and compiled into this work that has many wonderful memories from the best times of our awesome youth in old Ceylon.

Fazli Sameer/ 2020

Wellawatte Ways

Beginnings

Wellawatte, a small town in Colombo, lies immediately south of Bambalapitiya and is classified as zone 00600 within the Colombo Municipal region. The town begins at the old Dutch canal just before the Savoy Cinema and and extends all the way south to the same canal that spills into the sea just before the Hospital Road junction where Dehiwela begins.

It is bounded on the west by the magnificent waters of the Indian Ocean and extends to Pamankade where Havelock Road, forks and winds one of its ways to meet the Sri Saranankara Road bridge that stretches over the waters of the Dutch canal extending towards Kohuwela-Hospital Road junction on Dutugemunu Street.

Wellawatte has always been famous for its many eating houses, from the smalles corner vegetarian "dosa" joint to posh Chinese and European style restaurants, bakeries, and cafes.

The town has always been inhabited by a multicultural group of people since the sixties although in recent times the influx of a large number of Tamil people from the North has been significant.

Galle Road

The Savoy Cinema

The Savoy Cinema was owned by CV De Silva, who is said to have started life providing entertainment for overseas troops stationed in Colombo during World War II. It took its name from the more famous Savoy of London.

In the fifties, it was the scene of a commotion never seen in the annals of Sri Lankan cinema when the Savoy screened the 1956 musical film "Rock Around the Clock", featuring Bill Haley and the Comets, when many local boys attending the evening show got into a frenzy and started dancing inside the cinema hall.

The police had to be brought in to quell the situation as the poor fellows were deemed a nuisance to the rest of the audience.

Among the better-known films it showed in the 1960s were Gun Fever, Lady Chatterley's Lover and The Case against Brooklyn. The Savoy also screened the James Bond Movies Dr No, From Russia with Love, Goldfinger, and Thunderball, the first evening screenings of which were given to the Students Wing of the Ceylon Moor Youth League as benefit shows for fund raising.

Back in the 60s, it had usherettes, mainly women of Dutch Burgher descent, clad in white frocks and red and white dotted cravats with a torch in hand to show cinema-goers their seats, and who, during the intermission, would make another appearance holding trays filled with nuts, sweets and ice cream.

The gallery cost 55 cents, second class Rs 1.10, first class Rs 2.25. The Ordinary Dress Circle was Rs 2.75 and balcony Rs 3.60. There were Family Stalls for four at the rear of the hall, called Box Seats, costing Rs 4.50 per person.

The Savoy building, back then, had a mini bookshop in the foyer that sold a variety of comics, mainly Dell comics, with titles such as Roy Rogers and Lone Ranger.

There were also a row of shops in the building that faced Galle Road, including a clothes shop known as Himalayas run by a Sindhi family, and Savoy Emporium, which dealt in medicines and groceries.

The corner section sold customized ladies dresses on stitch/sew & wear basis. There was a Gents Hair Dressing Salon on the other side.

The Cinema has always been an icon that no one could ever miss. The stature of the building itself combined with the many attractive movies that were shown there could never be overlooked by anyone. Its location, right next to the Dutch Canal on the seaside, marks the beginning of the town. The de Silva family used to live on one of the many floors of the building and their daughter, Malkanthi, was a very popular and active young lady within the neighborhood.

The first floor housed a Chinese Restaurant which was frequented by thirsty young men in the dusky hours of the evening. A small car park that provided a reasonable facility to patrons circled the cinema from the canal end moving towards the rear and overflowing on to Charlemont Road.

pic by Tharindu Amunugama May 2012

The Cinema, has, in recent times been acquired by the Edirisinghe Group, owned and managed by EAP Edirisinghe, and refurbished with a new state of the art look, style, and features.

Why Layard's folly or Moda Ela?

The Wellawatte canal was not built by the Dutch despite the popular misconception. The canal was carved out in 1872 by the British as a flood outlet at Wellawatte. The road bridges of Wellawatte and Kirulaponne span this cut.

Carl Muller in his book Colombo has stated that the British Government Agent of the Western Province C.P. Layard, commissioned the undertaking of the canal.

However the plan seemed to have not worked out, for when the rain came it was found that the canal bed was considerably higher than the flood area. The hoped for drainage did not occur much to the disturbance of some and the amusement of others who dubbed the canal Layard's Folly. So, this is the story of its name.

Dhammarama Road

Right opposite the Savoy Cinema is Dhammarama Road, which runs along the Canal and veers its way towards Peterson Lane culminating at High Street, now called WA Silva Mawatha. The canal itself was an adventurous place for the kids of that era to splash in, catch ornamental guppies using sarongs, and spend their leisure hours wallowing in its murky waters that carried oil, waste, and many a spill from faraway places.

The Gauder's

It is related that all the land bordering Galle Road and the Railway tracks along the beach from The Savoy Cinema at the top of Charlemont Road to the Wellawatte Railway Station was once owned by a Burgher gentleman named Gauder. His children were named Charlemont (son), Alexandra (daughter) and Frances (daughter) after whom the successive streets have been named and stand that way to date. Not much information is available about the Gauder family.

Charlemont Road

pic by Tharindu Amunugama May 2012

Adjoining the Savoy, Charlemont Road, went straight down to the beach housing many a palatial residence and garden. The houses were all very large and spacious with sprawling flora everywhere. The street was the residence of many a rich and famous professional and businessman. The Rehmanjee's, a Borah family, lived on the left almost a block away from the Savoy. Sisters, Shireen, Themina and Batool lived with their Mum since the demise of their Dad some years before. Shireen married one of the boys down the street. Themina ran a small Montessori school in her garage but has since moved her residence and school to the bottom end of Station Road at Wellawatte in the premises of the Ariff residence.

The Rahumans lived a massive mansion on the right side of the street, almost three quarters of the way down to the beach. They belonged to the Memon community whose ancestors had arrived, long years ago, and settled as lucrative businessmen in Colombo. Their businesses were located mainly in the Pettah where they indulged in oilman stores, groceries, condiments, spices and other similar produce.

pic by Tharindu Amunugama May 2012

At the far end, on the left, lived Sulaiman Marikar-Bawa with his family in a massive house that had its semicircular bay windows facing the sea. The house had entrances from Charlemont Road and also the beach front. Sulaiman and his family used to provide night prayer facilities at his residence during the Islamic month of fasting (Ramadan) and a large gathering of believers from the locality used to patronize this service. He was a businessman and owned and managed his family textile business in the Fort called "Marikar Bawa's" who were very popular and famous for gentlemen's suiting and tailoring establishment, consisting of the finest fabrics imported from Europe. It was a tradition and privilege, in the old times, to have ones wedding suit purchased and tailored by Marikar Bawa's. Sulaiman was also a very charitable and philanthropic individual who was extremely generous to the poor and needy. A short, elderly man, sporting a spotless white beard he bore the personality and characteristics of a person who had seen some of the best times in life.

Moira MuthuKrishna (nee Van Cuylenburg), the pioneer in ladies hair dressing and beauty culture, opened her up her saloon, named "Moira's", down Charlemont Toad in the 60's and was patronized by most of the elite Colombo ladies from across all towns. She was married to Dinker MuthuKrishna and, after his death, to Pascoe. She passed away in Australia in September 2012. May she Rest in Peace!

email sent in by Asoka Weerasekera on Sep 28 2012:

VAN CUYLENBURG (Muthu Krishna/ Pascoe) – Moira (Salon Moira) – Cherished mother of Manjula, Prakash, Divaker and Omar, beloved sister of Pax Riedel, (late) Christine Van der Wall, Mystica Flamer-Caldera, Joyce Welle, Yvonne Poulier, (late) Heather Welle, Michael Van Cuylenburg and Derrick Van Cuylenburg, passed away peacefully on 23rd September in Perth Australia. A memorial service will be held in Colombo on 11th October at 5 pm at St. Theresa's, Thimbirigasyaya. Mystica 2697256/ Yvonne 072 – 5821361, Prakash +61407088235.

quote
Dear Fazli

The famous Muthukrishnas who owned Polytechnic, Dinkar Muthukrishna brother of Prabakar and his sister Mano was well known to me and my wife. In fact my wife learnt hair dressing under Moira.

She got married to a Pascoe after the death of Dinkar. She lived in Perth but we could not meet her there. She passed away. Kindly insert this in a suitable place in your blog.

Asoka
unquote

Names of some families who lived down this street are,

Adam
Sandy Austin
Dr Firazath Hussain
Hameed Jabbar Hussain
Athas Kuthdoos family
Moira Muthukrishna

Naleem Hajiar (Bairaha Farms/Naleemia Institute,
Beruwela)
Rehmanjee
Sulaiman Marikar Bawa

Sandy Austin in New Zealand wrote on FB:

"When I was a kid living in Wellawatte, Colombo, our neighbours were Uncle Percy and Aunty Jansz - that's what I called her. They were like second parents to me and I loved Aunty Jansz to bits. Followed her everywhere. Stayed with them during school holidays when they moved to Tickell Place in Borella. They had three children, Aubrey, Ralph and Camille and absorbed me into the family, giving me the love I lacked and desperately needed.

Little did I realise Aunty Jansz was Laura Adeline Vander Straaten Prins and related to me, Fae Egan(and the Austin clan) many times - the closest as our 4th cousin.

Aunty Jansz died in 1985 in Australia. RIP my lovely 'Mum'."

AGINCOURT

The Large House south of the Savoy was called AGINCOURT, it was occupied by the grandfather of Allister Bartholomeusz, Cecil Richard Lorensz Herft, retired Engineer PWD, Western or North Western Province.

C R L Herft was born on 13 Feb, 1860, in Manaar, and the name LORENSZ was given to him in honor of the great burgher personality of old times, Charles Ambrose Lorensz.

He had several children, Doreen Meynert (1898), Chapman Lorensz Meynert (1899), Cecil Eldred Meynert (1900), Idona Elspeth Meynert (1900), Lorenza Neomi Meynert (Oct 11 1901), Audrey Miriam Meynert (1903), Thelma Lilian Meynert (1904), Esmee Bertha Susanna Meynert (1908), Swinburne Annesley Meynert (1910)Fenton Vyville Meynert (1911), & Orville Wesley Meynert (1914).

Lorenza Neomi passed away during childbirth. Her daughter, Margeaux Lillian LOURENSZ is an eminent musician, ballet dancer, and artiste, who, presently (2006), lives in the UK. Esmee Bertha Susanna is the mother of Allister Bartholomeusz.

The HERFT family was a distinguished Family of NEGOMBO. C R L Herft was involved with the inauguration of NEWSTEAD COLLEGE, Negombo, a great Negombo School. He, along with St John Pereira, a Negombo resident, was responsible for the erection of the Bells of St Mary's in Negombo.

The Herft family home was named RIPPLEHURST and is now, the Kudapadu Police Station in Negombo. This was a haunted House, but the spirit was said to be a beautiful lady who tenderly sought the infants, if there were any. This is a well-known legend and Annesley Herft, uncle of Allister Bartholomeusz, Excise Superintendent had to present offerings at a ceremony, as traditionally demanded by local custom, to end this incident. (courtesy Allister Bartholomeusz, Melbourne, Victoria, Australia)

The Polytechnic

The Polytechnic or "Poly", as it was fondly referred to is said to be the first private Business College in Sri Lanka. Established in 1901 by Lawrie Muthu Krishna who was a pioneer in encouraging the youth to learn business and media skills, it was the pioneer training center in secretarial, typewriting, shorthand, book-keeping and other similar, basic, office management skills.

Later on the institute added many other attractive courses including, journalism, advertising, public relations etc in order to cater to changing demands of society.

The Poly was a place where youth were given an opportunity to pursue various vocations and careers, having left school and not having had the opportunity to pursue higher education or enter university. Those were days when shorthand and typing were necessary skills for the employment market and it was said to be the age of Pitman and Gregg.

The resulting clutter of the heavy old Remington Standard typewriters in the Polytechnic, added to Wellawatte's charms, and was referred to as the Charlemont Road symphony.

It was also one of the few, if not only, institutions, providing co-education where men and women sat together in the same classroom.

The Polytechnic grew from humble beginnings as a small private business college at San Sebastian Hill on Hulftsdorp to an establishment in Bambalapitiya and then to the present location in Wellawatte.

Lawrie Muthu Krishna's sisters Olive and Violet, having completed their commercial education at the Madras Technical College, joined their brother and were the Poly's first teachers.

The Poly was a place where the youth of Colombo used to meet, with the intent of pursuing various vocations and careers, having left school and not having had the opportunity to enter into university education or even pursue other higher levels of learning elsewhere. The institution, founded by Lawrie Muthu Krishna, way back in 1901, was the pioneer training center in secretarial, typewriting, shorthand, book-keeping and other similar, basic, office management skills. Later on the institute added many other attractive courses including, journalism, advertising, public relations etc in order to cater to the massive demands that these professions were exerting on the community for expertise.

The institution was located on the Galle Road, the second building from Charlemont Road, on the seaside and was monumental in its structure and echelon in that it portrayed a tremendous air of knowledge and camaraderie that was loved and cherished by many a young lad and lassie of that era.

The Muthu Krishna family belonged to the Colombo Chetty community, a group of people who originally migrated from Gujarat in India to the south and ended up on the western coastline of Sri Lanka, concentrating mainly in Colombo and its northern suburbs.

Kirthie Abeyesekera, a famous journalist who worked tirelessly for the Lake House Group of newspapers in Colombo, and who later taught journalism at the Poly, and subsequently migrated to Canada, where he spent his last days there until his demise a few years ago wrote about Poly in the Sunday Island of December 30, 2001 as follows:-

quote
Polytechnic celebrates 100 years of vocational and tertiary education in Sri Lanka

By Kirthie Abeyesekera, Sunday Island December 30, 2001---

Reflections on the Polytechnic at Wellawatte from distant Toronto in Canada, mirror a myriad images of an era gone by.

When Sharadha de Saram told me that her mother, Mano Muthu Krishna, would like me to make an editorial contribution for the Poly's centennial, it ignited dormant flames of a forgotten age.

I have to go back three decades to revive memories of the Poly, the Wellawatte landmark that has many a story to tell. My links with this age-old institution go back to the 'seventies. It was a decade of significant socio economic and political upheaval that changed the course of the country's history. At the turn of the decade, 1970 saw the fall of the Dudley Senanayake, United National Party government. The United Left Front led by Sirima Bandaranaike had ushered in a new social order widely acclaimed as the 'Peoples's Age.' For the first time, the country's ultra-Left movement had a voice in government.

The following year, some of the very forces that helped oust the right-wing, rose in open rebellion when the Janatha Vimukuthi Peramuna launched a nation-wide armed attack on the Establishment. To appease the youth yelling for social justice and economic emancipation, ceilings were set on incomes and landownership. Even the country's name was changed from 'Ceylon' to 'Sri Lanka,' to satisfy the nationalist revival call.

Two years later, the Associated Newspapers of Ceylon Ltd., better known as Lake House, which had been set on fire by the mob celebrating the 1970 election victory, was taken over by the government, striking a virtual death blow to the freedom of the Fourth Estate.

Amidst the chaos and turmoil that are the inevitable result of radical change, a few old institutions managed to survive. In 1973, Mano Muthu Krishna, a director of the Polytechnic edited the Women's Page of the 'Sunday Observer' I was working for at the time. Her brother, Dinkar, another director, endorsed his sister's choice of me. I had recently returned from the United Kingdom with a Diploma in Journalism which probably, prompted Mano to pick me to conduct the Poly's Journalism Course. My predecessors as lecturers had been Andrew de Silva, Ms. Fleming, a foreigner, Sita Parakrama and Reggie Michael.

Thus began my bi-weekly trek to the Poly amidst a hectic work schedule in crime reporting and feature writing. These visits gave me a closer look at a commercial institute that equipped men and women to face the realities of the working world.

'The Polytechnic Ltd.' was founded in 1901 by Lawrie Muthu Krishna, an imposing personality. He wore a long coat and waistcoat with winged collar. In keeping with the trend of his generation, he wore his hair long and, like all good Colombo Chetties, he always carried a folded, black umbrella. He was held in high esteem by the business community.
A man of broad vision, he realized the importance of tertiary and vocational education and catered to that need. It was a time when the country's educational system, based on academic study, was not geared to the realistic labor-market. From humble beginnings as a private business college at San Sebastian Hill on Hulftsdorp, Muthu Krishna set up the Polytechnic, first at Bambalapitiya and then at the present location in Wellawatte.

His sisters, Olive and Violet, having completed their commercial education at the Madras Technical College, joined their brother and were the Poly's first teachers. At the time, young women who had no interest in pursuing higher studies, found the Poly an ideal institution to hone skills mat would help them to be useful working members of the community, while building up their own careers. The Poly provided courses in communication skills, business correspondence, secretarial management, bookkeeping and accounting - all of which became popular, particularly with young ladies just out of secondary school.

The youngest pupil in my first Journalism Class was a 16-year-old girl from me Holy Family Convent, Bambalapitiya. My oldest student was a 58-year-old man on the eve of his retirement - a barometer of the wide age-group that comprised the Poly's students.

There were a few other academies and tutories scattered around the city. But the Poly stood out distinctively and was, by far, the most popular. The Poly was unique for two reasons. While other educational institutions were, by and large, denominational, the Poly was non-sectarian. It was also one of the few, if not only, institutions, providing co-education where men and women sat together in the same classroom. The Poly was also considered an alternative to university, and it became trendy for one to say, "I go to the Poly."

Of course, the Poly was also an excuse for teenagers to get out of their homes. Unsuspecting parents believed their offspring were preparing themselves for a career. But some of the romantically-inclined, playing truant, sought the 'Savoy' next door where matinee shows set the scene for stolen kisses.

Shadhara herself, has childhood memories of the institution founded by her forefathers. "I enjoyed my childhood, living next to the Poly," she says. "I loved to hear the gossip outside our home window which was always packed with Poly students. Of course, they didn't know I was listening."

Today, Poly students are scattered around the world, in many professions. I've met them in England and Australia. Many are here in Canada. They speak with warmth and affection of the friendships made in their Poly days which have endured over the years.

Some of my own journalism students are doing well in life. Firoze Sameer is a successful businessman and a prolific writer who has authored books, including a documentary on the infamous Ossie Corea - 'Dossier Corea.' One of my brightest young sparks, Lalani, the daughter of a former Permanent Secretary, C. J. Serasinghe, is now a legal secretary at the Ministry of Justice. She tells me, "The journalistic skills acquired under your training at the Poly come in very useful in my research presentations, editing legal publications, etc..

In many parts of the world, Sri Lankan expatriates, loyal to their 'Alma Mater,' have formed associations of Old Boys and Old Girls - Anandians, Nalandians, Royalists, Thomians, Bridgetians, Visakhians, Josephians, Peterites - the list is endless.

At home and abroad, men and women who have passed the portals of the Poly have entered me outside world, armed with confidence. As a tribute to their second 'Alma Mater' - if you will - these alumni should band themselves together and proudly proclaim themselves as 'Poly's Past Pupils.'

When the sexes meet, the inevitable happens. Romance fills the air. Love blossoms. Hearts meet. Partings leave broken hearts.

From ten thousand miles away, I send greetings to the Polys centennial celebrations, and would wish to conclude this editorial contribution on a personal note that had a happy ending.

My daughter, Chitra, on completing her secondary schooling at the Devi Balika Vidyalaya at Borella, took a secretarial course at the Poly, which landed her, her first job at Heath & Co. While at the Poly, she met Dev, a fellow-student. Their friendship grew. Later, Dev left for Canada to start a new life. Chitra followed him to take him for her life's partner.

Now, happily married for over a quarter century, and enjoying a stable family life, they have two University-educated daughters, Tamara and Dilani. Chitra herself has risen high in her profession as a banker.

In a real sense, the Poly is responsible for me and the rest of our family making our home in Canada. We followed Chitra instead of going to Australia which we had originally planned to make our home.

Unquote

Noel Crusz also wrote an interesting account of the Poly in the Sunday Times of Jan 6,2002 as follows:-

quote
The 'Poly' doors opened and in came the girls
By Noel Crusz , Sunday Times, Jan 6, 2002

It is a hundred years since Lawrie Muthu Krishna brought business skills to the masses. The 'baby boomers' told their husbands, "We will not be dictated to, and then thanks to The Polytechnic went on to become stenographers!" It was in 1901 that a young man had a vision that would spell a silent saga for thousands of men and women. He founded the first private Business College. Lawrie Muthu Krishna was a self-made man. He realized that in the narrow confines of academic education, the masses would be left out because they could not afford it, and neither had the inclination for university education.

As a teenager at St. Peter's College in 1939, I saw Lawrie enter the College gates with his sons Prabhakar and Dinkar. Lawrie was in his long white coat, trousers, waistcoat, winged collar and tie: almost a Dickensian character from a 19th century novel. He wore tortoise shell spectacles. His long hair ended in curls minus the sideburns. His black tightly furled umbrella, was the significant 'vade mecum' of the soft spoken Colombo Chetty community. The Rector of St. Peter's College, Fr. D.J. Nicholas Perera, and the Vice-Rector Fr. Basil Wiratunga informed Lawrie that his son Prabhakar had won the College "Open Essay Prize".

All of us were on the eve of World War II, and the commandeering of school buildings by the Allied Forces in Ceylon, faced new challenges. Lawrie Muthu Krishna was a pioneer in encouraging youth to learn business and media skills. He started in modest cramped buildings in San Sebastian Hill in Colombo 12. Maybe he saw the legal luminaries flocking to erect their offices near the Law Courts. Lawrie's vision worked overtime. It was founded on high spiritual and moral values. He saw the cut- throat commercial world invading accepted values. Soon he persuaded his sisters Olive and Violet to return to Ceylon from Madras. These young women had excelled in the Madras Technical College in commercial and media skills. They were to be the driving force in his tutorial staff, and a great asset to this family venture. This has been the backbone of the Polytechnic saga.

It has been a century of achievement spanning two World Wars plus a Depression and witnessing the first Boer War prisoners entraining for Diyatalawa. E.G. Money brought the first automobile to Ceylon, while Lawrie had a say when the first Sinhalese typewriter was produced in 1912. Before long, thousands would be tapping away on heavy manual typewriters. Colombo was bursting in the seams. There was an exodus from the over-populated city to the residential areas of the 'golden mile' from Colpetty to Wellawatte. The need for an established Business College, with a wide choice of vocational and tertiary education was part and parcel of Lawrie Muthu Krishna's vision. I still remember the clutter of the heavy old Remington Standard typewriters in the Polytechnic. It was known as the Charlemont Road symphony. The Galle Road had been widened, the Wellawatte bridge over the canal had been drained and re-built.

A generation of teenagers and school-leavers made a bee-line to the Polytechnic to hone their skills under Lawrie's supervision. It was the age of Pitman and Gregg where shorthand and typing were necessary skills for the employment market. There was a craze for commercial subjects, and business skills and accountancy.

The Government education system lagged miserably in spite of Lawrie Muthu Krishna's call for a re-orientation of media and communication skills.

With Wellawatte and Bambalapitiya and Colpetty South adding to the exodus into the 'Golden Mile', we saw crowds of young women, flocking to the Poly. The traditions of Holy Family Convent, St. Paul's Milagiriya, Lindsay Girls School were brought to the Poly classes. Parents felt safe in sending their daughters to learn shorthand, typing and accountancy under Lawrie and his professional staff, where the family was the backbone.

The branches at Fort and Wellawatte were a boon especially in a post-war world. Of course the 'Savoy Theatre' and the ice cream parlors of Alerics, Lion House, Paiva's and Dew Drop Inn added an element of romantic spice. When World War II broke out, hundreds of girls and young men, who learnt shorthand and typing were to be in clover on jobs with the Allied Command.

The Polytechnic Certificate was widely accepted, even in Australia and Canada. A Polytechnic product signified achievement and employers attested to this. The century of the Polytechnic Foundation is indeed an accolade to its founder. Lawrie Muthu Krishna had a heart of gold. He had a great love for his students. He was a pioneer in every sense. His firm of 'Public Accountants and Auditors' saw a wide clientele.

The Chatham Street offices at Negris Building (Fort) survived till the end of World War II. Lawrie did not stint in giving advice for a song and a cup of tea. Today accountants earn by the minute! I can still recall the day I saw Lawrie Muthu Krishna coming out of 'Collette Studio' in Bambalapitiya. We teenagers took our films for developing and printing and Mr. Collette (cartoonist Aubrey Collette's father) helped us. Lawrie too sought his help, to enlarge handwriting, when Lawrie was the only Private Examiner of Questioned Documents. No wonder handwritten legal documents and forgeries were grist for Lawrie's mill. The Poly was appointed to represent many UK examining bodies for recognized qualifications.

A hundred years for the Polytechnic are also a tribute to Olive and Violet, the Muthu Krishna sisters who were the real pioneers. Three generations have seen this Business University as alive and significant and up-to-date as ever. It has weathered political and economic storms. It brought in a new world of media and today with modern computer skills, there are giant strides. Prabhakar Muthu Krishna was in school at St. Peter's College with me. He was an athlete and a prolific reader. After his father's death he took over responsibilities with his equally talented brother Dinkar. Dinkar too inherited his father's skills, and also became an Examiner of Questioned Documents, besides being President of the Netball and Badminton Federation. Both brothers have passed away, Dinkar at 49 and Prabhakar at 50 and it was left to the sister Mano to bring the Institute to the stature of what it is today. The contribution of the siblings to the saga was significant.

The Poly reaped the business acumen of the Roches,

Machados, Carvallios, Paivas, F.X. Pereiras, Davoodbhoys, Sankar Ayers and De Liveras: firms that employed Poly girls. Mano, a product of Holy Family Convent, with contemporaries like Myrle Swan, was already making a significant contribution to the emerging new woman's world. A fair skinned, soft-spoken woman, Mano scooped many interviews of leading personalities, organized fashion and beauty contests, and ran the Poly with clocklike precision, notwithstanding her active fox terriers! Her own communication and broadcasting skills were lavishly shared with her pupils at the Institute. Mano as a journalist worked with me at the 'Davasa' under that charismatic Editor D.B. Dhanapala. It was she who broke the ice on the 'Boonwaat murder scoops.'

The Polytechnic centenary is a simple acknowledgement that the future of a country lies in the vision of its teachers, of its pioneers, of men and women of vision who saw the full spectrum. Lawrie Muthu Krishna saw the intense need of tapping the talent of the young, of helping them to perfect those skills that would help them in life. Little wonder that it was in the heart of his own family that he found his inspiration and achievement. There is no doubt that the Polytechnic has in a way molded the social fabric of Colombo South. The feminist movement and the Victorian ideals that woman's place was merely in the home was given a jolt. No wonder women rushed to learn typing skills at the Poly. The Centenary is no doubt a deserving accolade to the man, who played no small part in the Polytechnic saga.

Unquote

Isabelle Diana Pereira said: *"Did my secretarial studies at Polytechnic, Wellawatte".*

The Rilla Family

Abdul Rahman Mohamed Rilla lived in the adjacent plot. His sons were Rahim and Fazil Rilla. The daughters are Naleefa, Mazeeya, & Farahana. Mrs Rilla, Sithy Zahira Salih, was the sister of the famous building contractor, Rauf Salih, the Moors Sports Club cricketer Makkin Salih, Zacky Salih, and Sithy.

Dr Raffels Dispensary

Upali Obeyesekere: *Wellawatte also had a few private medical practitioners - Dr. Pinto and Dr. Samaranayake. Dr. NO was playing at Savoy and John was on his way when he met David who asked, "John are you doing to see Dr. NO?" John politely replied, "No, I am going to see Dr. Pinto". A joke from the sixties.*

Kshamalee Wirekoon: *Upali Obeyesekere nice joke. Anil and l lived on Peterson Lane, parallel to the canal when first married...his sister Charmaine and Francis were on Davidson Rd, close by. My parents were on Turret Rd... As a kid my father had a Savoy pass, knew CV de Silva, so we went to all the movies. All the Bill Hayley Rock n Roll movies were at Savoy...also many others. Loved the theater screen curtain, in fact, over here, bought a similar patterned dress! Those were the days! As the song says!*

Alexandra Road

The gram and nuts shop at the helm of this street was a very popular place where both young and old folks relished their bites.

Naleem Hajiar, the famous gem merchant and pioneer of the Bairaha poultry farm and industry, from Beruwela, moved in to establish his Colombo home down Alexandra Road.

MTM (Thaifoor) Hassim, son of WM Hassim and AJM Sadiq lived down this street, towards the far end, on the rightside walking west, closer to the Marine drive.

Annasamy and family, who ran General Metals Industries in Kelaniya, (Babujee, Sadasivan, Ramani, and rest of the family) also owned a large house down the street. Sadly, they had to leave Colombo and settle down in Tamil Nadu after the 1983 ethnic riots when their factory was burned to the ground.

The Abdul Cader family, of Rokeby Press fame, lived next door. Jameel (Jack) cader ran the press successfully at Union Place.

Kumar Kanagarajah, who worked for a bank in Colombo, also lived down this street. He has since migrated to Canada.

People who lived down this street, as shared by Saraswathi Ramarao in Chennai are:-

Abdul Cader (Rokeby Press, Jameel/Jack)
Adil
Fyroze
Fat Ramani
Kumar Kanagarajah
Chewing gum 😊...don't know his actual name!
Thaifoor Hassim and family
W.M.Abdul Jabbar
Zubair Naina Marikar
Sahal
H.L.M. Mohiideen
Najibudeen
S.L.M. Mohideen
A.M. Buhary
Bin Ahamed
Lolvani Samsudeen
Proctor Kanagarayan
Madihaparanam
Shanker Aiyyar, Babujee, Sada, Ramani
Helsingher
C. Nawaratnaraja Q.C.

The Kinross Swimming and Life Saving Club (KS&LSC)

On the Beach stood the Original KS&LSC – established in 1940 . This great Club produced several Champions in Swimming & Aquatics. The Club produced several outstanding spear fishermen and introduced the sport of spear fishing to Ceylon. To name a few, the legendary Gerd Von Dincklage, Ralph Forbes, Tissa "Saigon " Ariyaratne, Rodney Jonklaas, Hilmi Khalid, Turab Jafferjee, Langston Pereira, Ron Bartholomeusz, Hildon Bevan were all world class spear fishermen. Rodney Jonklaas was an authority on marine life. Rodney invited Sir Arthur C Clarke and his companions Mike Smith and Tony Buxton to explore the wrecks off the coast of Ceylon and film the magic of the sea and glorious reefs of this magic Isle. Rodney Jonklass was the Assistant Superintendent of the Colombo Zoo in the days when the Dehiwela Zoo was one of the best in the world, The Superintendent of the Zoo, the legendary Aubrey Weinman also had a close Bamba connection.

The Kinross bathing enclosure was situated opposite the site of the original KS&LSC. The enclosure was located in the sea. It consisted of two rafts and several orange barrels placed in a semi-circle, a relatively safe bathing area for both bathers and swimmers. This was the idea of Mr. Guy Thiedeman, a champion athlete – Municipal Playground instructor and Lifesaver who resided in the area. However, several incidents of drowning did occur which prompted Mike Sirimanne, who was a regular swimmer, to decide that it was necessary for the presence of Life Guards. Mike with the help of his close friends, Herbert Pathiwela, Elmo and Lou Spittel, Anton Selvam, Ron Kellar, Basil Misso, Hugh Stewart were the first life savers, who received their training from Guy Thiedeman and later on Harry

Nightingale, an Australian who introduced the Australian method of Surf Life Saving. This gave birth to the Kinross Life Saving Club in 1941. The club sought and obtained affiliation to the Royal Life Saving Society of U.K. and the Surf Life Saving Association of Australia. In the course of time the club ventured into competitive swimming and other aquatic sports and was named the Kinross Swimming and Life Saving Club with Guy Thiedeman the first President and Mike Sirimanne, the Legend of Kinross Club, General Secretary. The original HQ of the Club was a shack build by the founders on the beach opposite Kinross Avenue. The K.S & LSC soon became a byword in swimming and dominated the Two-Mile Sea Swims. Swim Champions Gerd Von Dincklage, Ralph Forbes, Hugh Stewart. Hilmi Khalid, Carlislie Chalon, Allister Bartholomeusz, Ian Kelly, Tony Williams (1960 Olympics) Desmond Templar, Rattan Mangharam, Randy Gray, Henry Perera, are names that come to mind. Other names who made significant contribution to the Club, were Tissa Ariyaratne, Gunaseelam Kanakratnam. Aubrey Van Cuylenberg (Water Polo, Ceylon Soccer goalkeeper), Langston and Fred Pereira.

In 1955, an improved clubhouse was built on the beach just opposite the Station. The club was built on the proceeds from the carnival, sponsored by Mr Thaha, which ran for about two months on vacant property owned by the William Pedris Family, free of Lease.

The Club was moderately damaged by the recent Tsunami and the present committee of management is hoping to restore the Club and improve the facilities for members.

Unfortunately due to changing situations the Club is not in the forefront of aquatics any more. The fierce competition and the "Spirit of Kinross" for which the Club was renowned in the period 1941 – 75, no longer exists, sadly.

Without Rodney Jonklaas former Assistant Superintendent of the Colombo Zoological Gardens at Allen Avenue, Dehiwela, original Member of Kinross Swimming & Life Saving Club, founder member of the Reef combers Spear fishing Club, the exploits of Arthur C Clarke & Mike Wilson would not reached the heights of underwater exploration in Ceylon. Aubrey Weinman was the Superintendent of the Zoo at that time which boasted to be one of the best in the world.

Other great world class divers/spear fishermen of that era were Langston Pereira, Gerard von Dincklage, Hilmi Khalid, Turab Jafferjee, Ron Bartholomeusz, Tissa Ariyaratne, Hugh Stewart, all of the KS&LSC, and Carlyle Ranasinghe, Authokarale. There is another UK contribution from Jimmy Buxton whose wife was the Norwegian beauty Gunilla Buxton.

Mention must be also made of the annual spear fishing competition between The KS&LSC and Reeefcombers for the Donavan Andree Challenge Cup.

Ralph Forbes (Chanko), was killed in a plane crash in about 1957- He was with the RCAF and was trained by the RAF in Cranwell UK.

Hilmi Khalid was an all-time Kinross great and without doubt a world class spear fishermen. He lived at the top of 5th Lane Kollupitiya. Hilmi now lives in LA, USA and deals in exports of tropical fish mainly from Sri Lanka.

Allister Bartholomeusz has known all the guys mentioned above including Dr Arthur C. Clarke. Allister is also referred to as "The Scribe" relative to all Aquatic Sport including Swimming, Waterpolo, Spear Fishing, and Surf Life Saving in the period 1949 – 1965.

The Wahab family

Cassim Wahab, the well known racing driver lived here. His family owned and managed the jewelry shop, "Bullion Exchange" at Bambalapitiya.

The Wellawatte Mosque

The Wellawatte Mosque was built by OLM Mohamed Cassim Marikar. His children are Reyal, Lafir, Azhar, Wazir, Sithy Sarifa (who was married to AMM Awn and after his death, Wapu Marikar Saleem), Ayeshathul Zuhurifa (wife of Sulaiman Marikar-Bawa), Arifathul Khaira (wife of Barrister AHM Salman) and Noor Zanooba (wife of ACM Mohideen).

Frances Road

The Nizar and Anver families lived down this street. The late Mushtaq Mahful, a very popular figure at the Kinross Club and diving for lobsters at night also lived down this street.

Hameedias

This was a small time textile and tailoring establishment in the 60s which has now grown into a huge mens fashion manufacturing and distribution enterprise spurred on by the sons of the founder.

GB de Pinto & Sons

A famous pharmacy that was patronized by the people living in Wellawatte.

Nanking Silk Store

Textile and gift boutique

HongKong Store

Gift Shop

Nooranis

Textiles

Station Road

The Colombo Gas & Water Company stood facing the Galle Road between Frances Road and Station Road. This enterprise supplied town gas for cooking to subscribed homes via gas pipelines laid underground on the street. Hameedia's and Hong-Kong Store stood next door.

The Haniffa's, Dr GR Muthumani's Dispensary, The Nizar's, DLM Faleels family, AC Noordeens family, MFA Marzook, Cook's, Ariff's, Ghouse Mahal and several other families lived down Station Road.

MHM Hussain, MHM Mueenudeen and MHM Ghouse are the three Haniffa brothers who have since moved out of the street. Hussain continued to live here but has also moved out since. Fareena Shahabdeen, the sister, married Ifham from Kandy and now lives at Dehiwela.

Feizal Nizar, Dr. M Fazli Nizar and Faiz Nizar lived next door moved to their own homes in other parts of Sri Lanka and the UK. Feizal passed away after a long illness while Fazli Nizar (Ward Place) and Faiz Nizar (UK) have also moved on. Their cousin Nina Esmerelda Mihilar also lived here until she moved to the UK later on.

Zuhair and Aziz Faleel lived with their parents before marrying and moving away to their spouses homes in Colombo. The old house was subsequently sold after the death of DLM Faleel, their father.

The Noordeens lived next door and their large home spanned the full width between Station Road and Lily Avenue. They too sold their home and moved to various other locations within the city of Colombo.

A long row of small adjacent houses came next leading all the way down the left side of Lily Avenue towards the sea.

The massive Ariff family home at No 10 has also now been blocked and divided amongst the children who have built their own homes on their respective plots. Jazeem has moved to Dharmapala Mawatha while Jazeed lives down 5th lane at Kollupitiya. Hamid married the daughter of the Mahuroof family and moved to Ridgeway Place where he passed away after a brief illness. Jamshed, married the daughter of MH Mohamed and moved to Bullers Road where he too passed away. The sisters Mehfuza, who married Farid Abdel Cader, and Khaneeza have moved out of Station Road since. Mehfuza passed away some years back.

Ghouse Mahal was sold to Aloysious Mudalali, who converted the massive mansion into a gambling club. Subsequently the property has been sold to a property development company who have now built up condominium apartment blocks on its facility.

MHM Ghouse, MHM Hussain, MHM Moinadeen, Fareena Shahabdeen
Dr Fazli Nizar, Faizal Nizar, Faiz Nizar, Dr Fawzia Sivardeen
Dr GR Muthumani, Dr Rosemary Muttumani
DLM Faleel, Zuhair Faleel & Azeez Faleel
Nagoor Pitchai, Shibly & Nazim
AMM Marzook, Suhail, Zaneera Shariff
Hassan Ghouse (Ghouse Mahal)
Ziyard Ghouse
AJM Ariff, Jazeem, Mehfuza, Jazeed, Hamid, Jamshed, Jihad

The Wellawatte Railway Station

pic by Tharindu Amunugama May 2012

Lily Avenue

Between Station Road and Lily Avenue is located the public toilets of the town. Several small to medium business establishments line the Galle Road and the Wellawatte Post Office spans the right side of Lily Avenue, facing the Galle Road.

Right at the helm of Lily Avenue, on the Galle Road intersection, was the back door entrance of Mirbaha Stores, a famous hardware store which had everything and was accessible after closing time of their Galle road frontage. It used to be remarked, jokingly, that Mirbaha Stores, run by South Indians, virtually had almost every stuff under the sun only lacked sale of a "father and mother"

The Sameer's moved to Wellawatte in the 1920s. A part of the family, subsequently, moved to Bambalapitya in the forties. The oldest son in law, AWM Ghouse, married Rameela Sameer and came as a Bridegroom from Old Moor Street in 1937 to No. 51 Lily Avenue, Wellawatte.

Rameela Ghouse (nee Sameer) attended St Clare's Wellawatte in 1919. The Sameer boys, Thahir, Farook, Ismail, and Sadiq, first attended St. Lawrence's School, opposite Lily Avenue in Wellawatte. Rameela has mentioned that the famous Royal College cricket captain, D.W.L. Lieversz (former GM Electricity Board) was her class mate at St. Clare's and the Principal at that time was Miss Marshall. Miss Marshal went on to start a school called Marshal Preparatory School.

Haji Ismail Effendi, the Islamic scholar and Moor Traveller, used to travel to Wellawatte to see his sons Sameer and Anis at Lily Avenue, and it was during one of these visits that he met with an accident while boarding the train at Wellawatte Station and passed away.

When the Sameer's moved to Station Road at Wellawatte there were hardly any houses in the town as it was considered then an outpost. From "Clifton House" at Station Road they moved in the twenties to Lily Avenue where Mr. Sameer built two houses at No's 43 and 45.

Mohamed Sameer's eldest son, Thahir, attended Royal College Colombo and he used to ply to school by rickshaw.

No 43 Lily Avenue was rented to Austin Silva, a top personality at Lake House and a strong Buddhist. Austin was married to a Burmese Lady called Doula. The Sameer's lived next door at No 45 Lily Avenue. Austin Silva used to send a few eggs to the Sameer's, daily, requesting them to break it for his family. He used to say that as a Buddhist he cannot commit the crime of taking a possible life the egg could produce, so he gave that task to the Sameer's to do it knowing it's not a sin in Islam. Austin had a few sons who also attended Royal College, the more famous of them being a Cricket Captain in 1951, Ubhaya De Silva. The others were Chula and Tilak, who were both icons at basketball at Royal.

Even during the war the Sameer's stayed at No 51 Lily Avenue and when the bombing took place they took cover in Aluthgama. After the Japanese air raid and WW2 was at the tail end they moved from Wellawatte to Bambalapitiya.

The popular Skyline Restaurant and Bakery sprung up just before the Post Office on the Galle Road and thrived very popularly during the seventies. However the business has now been closed and a huge bank building occupies its location.

The Mahadeva's, father who was a well known icon in The Pettah in the textile industry, sons Arjan, Baba, Cumiyan, Dhayalan, Ganendran, Hariputran, & Ilangowan, the Selvaratnam's (ex HM Customs), SHM Ghouse, Ms Poulier (who ran a nursery school which was attended by many a prominent man and woman of today), AWM Ghouse, MM Sheriff, The Fernando's, AJM Ariff, Dr. Arunachalam, Dr.Ekanayake, whose son attended St Thomas' Colege, Mt Lavinia, Mr Nalliah, a teacher at

Royal Primary School, Koneswaran, who also attended Royal and the Medical Faculty in Colombo, were some of the families who lived down this street.

The Koneswaran's have moved to Connecticut in the USA where he and his wife both practice as Cardiologists.

Ms Poulier's pre school, run by Mrs Dick (nee Poulier) stood at No 41. This school located in a garage attracted many kids in the nearby towns, many of them ending up in the high echelons in the Private sector. Ms Poulier was a charming Burgher lady who was married to a Scotsman, a grumpy old man with plenty of Colonial airs, a retired Engine driver during British Times.They used to go for evening strolls hand in hand and she wore a dainty hat and dressed in frilled dress and old man Dick in baggy cap and overall, carrying an umbrella.

He was always snorting away at the "natives' not giving them even an evening nod. She, for her part, was a smiling frail lady throwing in "good evening" at every passer by.

In the last house on the left lived a pretty lady named Sheila de Alwis who was married to Malcolm de Alwis. They had two children, Chrishanta who played cricket for St Peters' College and Shanthini, now domiciled in France.

A "Dara Maduwa" (firewood shop) spanned the left side of the street close to the Galle Road and this enterprtise served many a home with firewood for their hearths in those times when cooking gas and electric cookers were sci-fi only. Haleema Drapery Stores adorned the corner of Lily Avenue and Galle Road and survives, to date, as we speak.

A quaint little bookshop started by Mr Zakariya in the 60s and that went on to serve the community with a grand array of school books, work books, novels, comics and gift items. The shop was continued by his son Rizwie after him and went on to survive for more than a 100 years. Was previously Zachariah Bookshop. We used to buy our school books and stationery from here.

Collingwood Place

Names of some of the people who lived down this street are,
Dr. MSM Waffan
MSM Zarook

Hamers Avenue

Earnest, Rajah, Raina and Ghandi MacIntyre, lived down this street. They belong to the Burgher community who originally lived in Jaffna.

Nira Ponniah wrote on FB on May 19, 2020:
Harmers Place a by-lane we called it then had an intimate mix of families who lived there for decades. We knew each other's achi, seeya, periyapppah, uncle , nona and the list goes on. Cricket, badminton down the lane. Carom, 304, 532 to name a few.

If my dad's Fiat car wouldn't start all my neighbours came to push!! Mr . Reids's garden had every plant on earth including coffee beans. Rest of the families down Harmers Avenue were like extended family. You couldn't do a mischief my parents would come to know !

An extension of the neighbourhood then at Methodist College. We saw no difference in any one. What beautiful memories.

Times have changed. So sadly only one of our original neighbours remain in Harmers place now. Thank God for technology I am in touch with some of my neighbours and almost all my classmates. Praise the Lord.

The Wellawatte Police Station

Nelson Place
M Lareef

Adjward Hashim, Mackie Hashim, Faizer Hashim
(Gundara)

The Royal Bakery

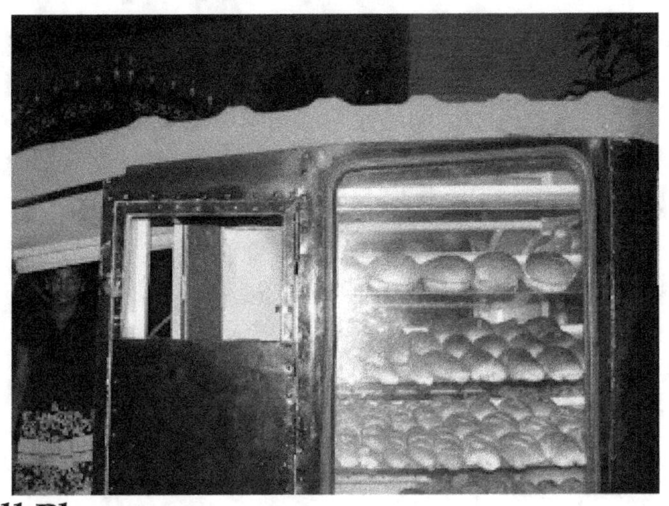

Boswell Place

Najumudeen, Iqbal & Farook
AHM Junaid

Gandhi Lodge

An enterprising vegetarian restaurant patroniozed by everyone who relished south Indian dishes. Dosa & Vada were the hot favorites at any time of day or night.

Moor Road

The Mohideen family along with the Bary's lived here. There were only three Moor families during the late 50s.

The Rudra Chamara was a good land mark for people who visited to get a night meal.

Don Charles Furniture hire, at the corner of Galle Road, was a well known timber and furniture joint now replaced by the Cargills outlet.

Delmon hospital has also sprung up along the Galle Road.

Major AMM Nazik and family also lived down this street.

Fernando Road

Vaverset Place

International Buddhist Center Road

36th Lane

Rajasinghe Road

A.K.M. Mohideen

40th Lane

41 Lane (Dr. EA Cooray Mawatha)
Hameed family, Fuzuli, Fenuzi
Proctor Thassim & Family

The public bathing well which we used to use on festival days was also located down this street. We used to enjoy taking a bath there in the concrete block tanks with our maternal grandpa, Rasheed Appa, who used to take us there.

42nd Lane

   Mario Pieris: *42nd Lane for me!*

Upali Obeyesekere: *Mario, I had two classmates on 42nd Lane. Dulip Jayamaha and Chandra Fernando (former IGP).*

Vivekananda Road

Rasheed (Singer Company)

Dr Visvalingam (WHO), Navindran (Royal College '59 Group)

Vivekananda Avenue

Ramakrishna Avenue

Somagiri Place

Ramakrishna Road

Babujee, N Sadasivan, Jayanthi, Sachu, Eshu
Myown Mustafa

Ramakrishna Mission

The main center of the Ramakrishna Mission is on Ramakrishna Road, Wellawatte.

The concept of a Ramakrishna movement in Sri Lanka started with the arrival of Swami Vivekananda in January 1897 on his way back to India after his historic address in the parliament of Religions at Chicago.

At the request of devotees he sent one of his brother disciples in July 1897 to Colombo to spread the message of Sri Ramakrishna.

The mission started its activities in the Island in 1924 with the management of a few schools.

The Ashrama building has a shrine, meditation and prayer hall, an administration section and book-sales department.

The shrine room is a hexagonal shaped construction where in the 'Sanctum Sanctorium' is enshrined a portion of the sacred Holy Ashes of Bhagavan Sri Ramakrishna Paramahamsa.

A Rig Veda dictum "Ekam Sat Vipra Bahudha Vathanthi" in Sanskrit with an English translation "Truth is one, Sages call it by various Names" are inscribed on the wall above the altar.

A separate building houses the library, reading room and a lecture cum prayer hall.

In addition, there is an auditorium named Swami Vivekananda Centenary Memorial Hall and an International Cultural Centre referred to as 'Guest House.'

Roxy Gardens

The late Ronnie de Silva, ex Chartered Bank, and his wife Pam (from the Bambalapitiya Flats) lived down this street.

**47th Lane
Rudra Park**

The Land Side

Wellawatte Bridge

Dhammarama Road

On the left of Dhammarama Road stood the Wellawatte Canal, bordering St. Peters College on the other side of its bank, and ran all the way up to the Wellawatte Spinning & Weaving Mills along Havelock Road. Many properties on the right side were owned and resided upon by members of the W M Hassim family.

The Bartels family lived here. Russel played cricket for BRC and Susan attended Lindsay Girls School at Bambalapitiya in the 60s.

ALERICS ICE CREAM

In 1949, when Aleric De Silva Wimalaratna ventured into ice cream, he wouldn't have dreamed that his family-run business will one day become a legend. Mr. Wimalaratna who studied and lived in Australia returned to Sri Lanka in the late 1940s with the intention of launching a business.

He capitalized on his expertise and knowledge gained in Australia in the field of ice cream manufacturing to start an ice cream manufacturing plant in Wellawatta.

Initially the ice cream made in his plant was sold by Mr. Wimalaratna himself and subsequently he entered the retail market of Colombo and down south. This was done through ice cream vans which sold Alerics Ice Cream at public places such as playgrounds, religious places, carnivals, etc. With its tender taste and distinctive look, Alerics became an instant favorite especially perfect for cooling down during a hot day. In 1949, sold a very popular 'ice chock' as well as a 'family block', which contained three flavours of ice cream, housed in a cardboard box

The brand's pure and natural taste had sealed its position as the nation's favorite. The business celebrated its success by opening the very first Ice Cream Parlour called Piccadilly Café in Wellawatta which was one of the most exclusive hang-out places in the 1960s.

In the 60s and 70s, it was one of the best known brands, where Alerics saw its golden era both as a comfort food and festive treat. The vanilla was a consolation for a minor disappointment, and chocolate was a reward for reaching a personal goal. But the company failed to maintain the momentum in the wake of strong marketing campaigns of major scale ice cream manufacturers. Despite losing its market share for other popular brands in the organized market, Alerics continued to operate mostly in rural areas and temples in and around Colombo through their distributor vans.

Roel Raymond and Others /May 2020

Posted by **Hinaya Ariff** on FB on Oct 31, 2020

"Ok a story Anno sorry. My cuz Anna took Manel n me for ice cream but actually she was sneaking out to meet her boyfriend which she had quite a number of cos she was so damn gorgeous She left Manel myself and asked to eat ice cream until they went for a drive n omg we were little. We whacked the ice creams n she freaked out when she came back n seeing the bill. Ha ha.
Anno let the car out of the bag after decades."

Frederika Road

The Mansoors, of whom Imthiaz and Rizvi were bankers, lived down this street. Opposite their home, on the right were the Bathusha family with their children, Rumi, Rifath, Reza, Razia, and Ruzna.

Naufal Abdul Rahman and his parents also lived here. Naufal married Fathia (Asma) Rahman from Hultsdorf.

Mohamadiya Hotel

Nimal Dias Jayasinha: Oh Muhammadiya Hotel and their ' fish bis-stake ' .....what wonderful times

Upali Obeyesekere: *Memories of City Motorways boarding house at #46 Galle Rd, Wellawatte right opposite Muhamadhiya Hotel.*

My brother Susantha and I had the front room in this chummery that housed many bank employees, govt servants and us. Manager was Mr. Eric Ranchigoda, a good friend of my late father.

Our room was the epicentre of many an evening party with music much to the dismay of a few of the boarders. For dinner, we just cross the road to Muhamadhiya for Egg Hoppers and Gothamba Roti. One of the happiest two years spent in Sri Lanka before emigrating to Canada.

Peterson Lane

The street that links Frederika Road to High Street

Kokila Road

1st Chapel Lane

2nd Chapel Lane

St. Lawrence's School

A missionary Catholic school who catered to girls education

W A Silva Mawatha (High Street)

A busy and sprawling street that ran all the way down, inland, to meet Havelock Road branching off towards Kalyani Road. The Abdul Rahman's lived in a massive mansion on the left. The home is now neglected and used as a hostel for students and visitors to the city.

Suvisuddharama Road

The street, adjoining the Sapphire Theatre, that begins at High Street and wends it way back to Havelock Road.

Shaharan Saleem, Thasneen, Imran, & Ummu lived down this street right behind the theatre. Hussain & Numa, Zain Naina Marikar, Moin & Ayesha & families also lived down this way.

Hampden Lane

The street that connects WA Silva Mawatha to Canal Lane running parallel to the Galle Road intersecting many other landside streets between the Wellawatte Market and Pennycuick Road.

Between Madangahawatte and Arethusa were the twin-houses of the Vander Hoeven brothers - the one on the right was where Melba, Sonna and Christine lived with their father. I can't remember the names of the other Vander Hoeven family.

Next to them and at the very bottom of Arethusa Lane was the bare block of land where the Baas (who owned the kadé) tethered his cows. Later on, the youngest Jayamanne daughter (Dulcie) built a Montessori School on this land.

Baas' Kadé was the local café for the residents of the Alakandiya. I remember that my parents had a tab at the Kadé for their cigarettes. This was also the firewood depot for the neighbourhood. There were almost always disagreements about the actual weight and volume of the firewood as obviously wet timber was heavier than the dry. The house next to the kadé was where the Pollocks family lived and I remember the tock-tock of Joyce Pollocks' high-heel shoes as she walked up or down Arethusa Lane.

This is a tribute to the baby-boomers of the area – Heather Gallwey, Mohan Coomaraswamy and his siblings, Bala Kanagaratnam, Sonna & Christine Vander Hoeven, Cedric, Bryce & Christine Fernando, Christopher, Evans & Karyn Pereira, Honourine Abeykoon, Ranjit & Siri Jayatunga-Perera, David, Ranil, Michael & Sharmini Goonawardene, Ivan, Anne & Paul Martinus, late Harsha Abeywardene, Shirley-Joan Bartholomeusz and her siblings, Fran Bartholomeusz, Janaka & Harsha Wijetunge, Janaka Rasiah, Kumar and Nedra Wagiswara, Rohan & Nilanthi Jayaratne, the Chuganis, Shantha & Chandra Wijeyrajah, Claude & Cheryl Wickeremasinghe, Suraj Perera and his siblings, Davanel & Radcliffe Flanderka, the Muhseens, Aloma Peiris, and the Sinnathamby girls…………possibly many others whose names I can't remember, though I can picture their faces. I wonder where life has taken them?

Manning Place

The Kirulaponne bus station (143)
Clay Pot /Coir mat shop

MOH Maternity Clinic
Chicken Market
M.S.M. Zackariya and Family
M.P.M. Hameed
M. Zubair
M.S.M. Riyal Hajiar
Nizam Mohamed
Sufi Ismail

The Wellawatte Market

I lived down a small lane that had no name, a few yards south of the Wellawatte market. It was right beside Elephant House on the land side and there were only 3 houses   down   it.

The Pereira's lived at 253/1 Galled Road. It was the last house down the lane. The head of the household was Dodwell (Bunny) Pereira. His wife was Lilian Pereira (nee Dabrera). They had three boys, Dodwell, Mark and George. Dodwell and Mark now reside in Australia and George is in Canada. Bunny died in 1961 after having suffered a stroke 9 years earlier. Lilian died in Canada in 1987.

The next house was 253/2 where the DeMel family lived. His name was Artie and he worked at the Education Ministry. His wife's name skips my mind. They had one daughter named Lynette.

Next to them at 253/3 were the Labrooy family. There was Neil who was married to Marjorie. The children were Skipper, Janice, Rodney, Cheryl and Brendan. They moved to Australia.

Next door to the Labrooy's house was the building that housed Elephant House and a few other stores. People lived above these stores and the entrance to their homes was from behind the building down the lane.

At the very top of the lane, right at the Galle Road there was the "jak woman". She had a little hut where she lived day and night and sold jak fruit on the pavement. No one knew where she got the jak from but it would be there fresh each day.

Next to this lane (closer to the Wellawatte Municipal market) there was another small lane that housed the "kammala" where they had a forge and used to put new wheels on bullock carts. At the top of this lane was a small store that sold everything. He had pencils, pens, stationery, erasers, etc. Everything one would need for school as well as toys and other paraphernalia. He was called Free Man. We would go into the store and take whatever we wanted and never had to pay for it. It was until later in life that my mother told me that "Free" Man would see on the street and she would have to pay for what we took.

Adjacent to Free Man was the shoe maker. We used to go into his shop and chat for an hour or so and watch him make and repair shoes. I still remember the green hued glue that he used to fasten the soles to the shoes.

On the pavement on Gale Road there were assorted vendors selling everything from fish to spices. We knew all of them and they used to keep an eye on us when we were very young that we didn't stray too far from home.

Sent in by George

George S. Pereira, Toronto, Canada

Fussels Lane

AC Deane, Siddiq Deane, Haniffa Deane, Ameena Deane

Naeem Samsudeen, Rauff

32nd Lane

S Gulasekharam (ex Chartered Bank)

Meimoona Adamaly

Mubarak Family, Noor, Muaz, Mueez

33rd Lane

55th Lane

St. Lawrence Road

At No 12 lived Carl Thiedeman and his family. Carl worked for Collettes Ltd in Colombo. His daughter Beverly is married to Mervyn Direcze of Lorensz Road, Bambalapitiya.

The Martenstyns lived at No 18.

Further down lived the Junaid family, the oldest daughter Mazeena marrying Ahmed Farooq Sameer of 298 Galle Road, Bambalapitiya. The other members of the family are Husain, Shamil, Navvar, Safi, and Serry.

On the left side lived Proctor Nawaz Ibrahim and his family.

> **Kumar Hiranandani:** *Used to live in St. Lawrence Rd. which is bang opposite Royal Bakery. People use to his bread baking oven to bake cakes. He used to charge 25 cts a tray. Gandhi Lodge was a small Dosa joint. Nothing great but cheap. There was a confectionary shop called Pudding House. Savoy was a nice theatre. Wellawatte was a nice laid back place*

Mrs. Junaid
Mrs. Haniffa

Rudra Mawatha

The Haniffa family lived down this street. Dr Naas and Dr Naalir are the sons.

THE MOREIRA FAMILY

The Moreira Family moved to No: 3 Rudra Mawatha from the Ceylon Electricity flats at Gas Works Street next to the Central Bus Depot due to Dad's promotion. The family consisted of Douglas, Fortune & siblings Adrienne, Diana, Christopher, Beverley, Geoffrey and Anne-Marie all residing in Australia now except for the passing away of Dad & Mum.

The move was much anticipated as we all were exited at new surroundings, new friends, smells and a new church being St Lawrence's on Galle road. We joined other Catholic worshippers of a Sunday walking in unison chatting, exited, skipping on our feet, local gossip etc: for Mass and Communion & then joining for lunch with usual feast of rice and curry..Sundays were always spent at Kinross for most of the day playing table tennis, life-saving duties as a volunteer, hot kadalay (gram) in a paper cone, cut pineapple and of course the cursery glances at the pretty girls !! Wonderful lazy days that still brings nostalgic memories & tears with peace and harmony with all ethnic people laughing and chatting.

The evenings was spent with visitors Brian Pereira known as Buri and Neville Overlunde listening to the Maliban Talent Quest on Radio Ceylon and picking the winners.

I attended St Joseph's College in Maradana after cycling to Otters swimming club down Bullers road for training for about 1-2 hours, sometimes having set the alarm clock incorrectly and arriving at Otters at 2am sleeping in one of the many couches near the bar. Dad was on a roster attending to the various malfunctions of electricity distribution along the many roads around Wella, Bamba etc:

I visited Ceylon / Sri Lanka in 1999 after 25 years migrating in 1973 and No:3 just looked the same where I climbed the gate pillar and reminisced wonderful memories often with tears in my years..Such good times!!!

I am visiting SriLanka once again in August 2011 to view progress, the social relationships amongst all ethnic groups, Uncle Brian & Aunty Joan Forbes of 14 Kalyani Road, Nigel and Karen now married..More gossip, curry, pappadams, wattalapan, love cake, Arro and much laughter & memories..

May the mighty Ceylon / Sri Lanka prosper with Dignity, Compassion, Tolerance, Love, Integretion of all ethnic people to be an example to mankind. I wish all people of my motherland Gods wonderful blessing and a long and happy life.

Geoffrey Moreira
Australia
Kiwi.boy1@bigpond.com

57th Lane

**A TRIBUTE TO THE FAMILIES OF
ARETHUSA LANE, MADANGAHAWATTE
LANE &
THE CANAL END OF HAMPDEN LANE**
sent in to the blog by Jennifer de Silva in Australia

What wonderful memories of those carefree days in Arethusa Lane – the boys playing cricket on the weekends and school holidays, the whistle of the Borakakul Karaya (man on stilts dressed as a woman) as he made his rounds, the Sakkili Band waking everyone up from their post-Christmas Lunch siesta. As I write this I can almost hear the end of shift siren from the Wellawatte Spinning & Weaving Mills (the redi molay nalawa) which you could set your watch by.

Who can forget the Paang Karaya from Royal Bakery with his load of bread, cakes, and Mas and Maalu Paang, vendors of fish, salt, coconut oil, vinegar, plantains, and anything that could be carried in a pingo (kadha karaya) or a basket on the head. Then there was the Thorombol Karaya with boxes full of all sorts of goodies from brassieres, to thread, nail polish, buttons, zips, lace, and ribbon – the list was endless, the Crab (Mud Crabs) Man who came from Negombo and the ice cream men from all the different companies (some good, some bad). On the weekends we would wait patiently for the woman who came around with Thalagulli, Halapa, Lavariya and Seenakku and other tiffin-time delicacies. We must not forget the lunch-boys on their bicycles who collected lunches from home and delivered it at school and work. "Rattu", the tall and lanky Tamil with the red turban and white sarong was the most famous among them.

In those days, you only needed to go to the market to buy beef and other perishable items and then one would go to Swastikas, Colombo Stores or Sri Mahal. Kerosene and firewood were all delivered to your door. There was even a draper who came round pulling a large cart filled with fabric for dresses, sarees, etc. When one did go to the market, the return journey was usually by rickshaw. Alas rickshaws are a mode of transport no longer used. I wonder what happened to the sons and grandsons of those old Rickshaw Men?

In the very early 1950's, the Canal was clean and I am told that boats used to come down from Piliyandala and beyond with vegetables and fruit to supply the Wellawatte and Dehiwela markets. Of course the canal became stagnant and almost disappeared after the shanty town came up. The men made a living by doing odd jobs, while the womenfolk worked as domestic aids in the houses of the area or made hoppers, stringhoppers and pittu for sale. I remember waking up in the morning to the sound of my mother's voice telling off the hopper boy from the Alakandiya, because he was late or the hoppers were not up to scratch. One resident of the alakandiya was Anula Karunatillake, a Sinhala film star.

Anula became famous when a photo of her crossing the canal on her way home from school was published in a newspaper. Anula was a popular actress and continued to live with her family (her parents were vendors at the Wellawatte Market) at the "alakandiya" (canal) until her marriage to the cameraman who took that photo.

Arethusa Lane

Arethusa Lane was an example of multiculturalism – Sinhalese, Burghers, Muslims, Tamils, Indians (Southern and Northern) all co-habiting peacefully. Even the 1958 riots didn't affect this little cul-de-sac because we looked out for each other. We shared each other's religious festivals and the associated food – the delicious Buriyani and Wattalappam at Ramazan, Kavum, Kokis and Kiribath at Sinhala New Year, Pongal Rice, Boondhi, Halva at Thai Pongal and Deepavali. Not forgetting the Christmas Cake, Cream Crackers and Kraft Cheese washed down with Ginger Beer/Milk Wine during Christmas.

Arethusa Lane was very narrow and one vehicle had to pull into a gate way to let the other pass. Now, it is even narrower, with houses built up to the edge of the road and surrounded by high walls with metal gates. Most of the houses are unrecognisable and I had to close my eyes to remember Arethusa Lane as it was in the 1950's to the 1970's and only then was I able to imagine the former residents many of whom have past away, moved elsewhere or migrated. It also brought to mind the birthday parties, New Year's Eve get-togethers and last but not least the games of cricket played on Uncle's badminton court even though girls were not included.

Now I have to reach down to the deepest recess of my mind to gather the names of the families. From the top of the Lane going down on the left – Wickremasinghe, Abeywardene, De La Harpe the De Kretser flats whose residents included Poulier, Forbes, De Kretser, Peiris, Van Langenberg, de la Zilva, Cooke, and Ching. Next house down was the Weeramantry house. Joyce Weeramantry married Osmund Jayaratne (later Professor of Physics). Meetings of the pre-coalition LSSP took place on the veranda of this house and many an LLSP election manifesto was drawn up at these meetings.

The big house at the top of Madangahawatte Lane belonged to Gate Mudaliyar Wickremasinghe. Of course, we must not forget Mr Nicolle who lived on the other side of Madangahawatte Lane and the various families that lived in his annexe – Smith, Candappa, and others. Next down was Flanderka, Wijetunge, Ferdinands/Chapman, Pereira, Abeysekera. Mr & Mrs Abeysekera were killed in a car accident around 1960. At No. 31 was the Jayamanne family and the Gallweys who lived in their annexe. No. 33 was where Professor EOE Pereira and his family lived. Lorenz (Lollo captained Royal in 1954) and Brian played cricket for Royal. The last house on the left was the old house on the big block where the Bartholomeusz family lived. This was a quaint house and I remember playing with Shirley Joan and her brothers in the large garden. In the 1960's after the family had migrated to Australia, the house was pulled down and a block of flats came up on the site which later became the home of the Develo Radio Company.

In the days prior to house ownership restrictions, house numbers 23 to 33 were owned by Mr Jayamanne, who lived in a large house on Galle Road near the Dehiwela Bridge.

Going up the lane from the bottom was the house of the Perera's where "Uncle" lovingly tended his badminton court. Next was Fernando and two houses up was Kanagaratnam. No. 40 was Proctor Douglas Silva and at No. 38 the Goonewardene family (a daughter of Gate Mudaliyar Wickremasinghe). At No. 36 in those early days of my memory, lived the Krishnamurthy family. They were South Indian Brahmins and I can still smell the Thosais, Vadais, Rasam and other vegetarian delights prepared by Mrs K and her two older daughters. Later on, the house was renovated by the Illesinghe family; Mrs Illesinghe (Geraldine) being the oldest of Gate Mudaliyar Wicksremasinghe's daughters. The Razzaks lived at No 35. The next house, an original of the area, was where the Martinus brothers lived with their sister. In the house next to them lived Kenneth (their younger brother) and Peggy Martinus. Next up was the house in which the Ibrahim family lived. A school friend Thahani Marzook was part of this family as were the Muhseens who built the two town-houses next door. When the Ibrahims moved out, the Chithambara Nadar family moved in. The Muhseen town-houses were occupied by the Musheens (and later on Dr Samaranayake, the famous gynaecologist, and his family) and the Chuganis who owned Luxmi Silk Stores in the Fort. Vimoo and Nimoo Chugani attended St Pauls Milagiriya School at Bambalapitiya. Next up was the house owned by Gerry Karunatillake, next door was the house where the Grabbos lived and after they migrated the house was renovated and the Sinnathamby family moved in.

Across from the De Kretser flats lived the Brohier family at No 14 – a daughter, Lavender married Freddy White. Then the other Abeywardene family – son Harsha was the General Secretary of the UNP and was killed in a car bomb attack on High Street (WA Silva Mawatha) in the 1990s.

At the top end the residents included Cockburn, FXC Pereira, Barr-Kumarakulasinghe and at the very top where Hotel Sapphire now is, was the BER Cooray family. Mr Cooray later purchased the Cockburn house. There were also the large family of Josephs; Mr Joseph was the Church Appu at the Dutch Reformed Church at the top of Arethusa Lane.

Isabelle Diana Pereira: *My Dads people were from Pereira Lane/Arethusa Lane.*

Madangahawatte Lane

My mother who was born and bred in Wellawatte, told us that in the mid 1900s, this was a forest of Madang trees which they used to walk through to play with their friends, the daughters of Mr Pereira (after whom Pereira Lane is now named) and the father of Professor EOE Pereira. Madangahawatte Lane's residents included Balaji, Wagiswara, Pereira (Christopher was an Announcer at the SLBC), Abeykoon, Wickremasinghe, Martenstyn, Fernando (Cedric, Bryce and Christine), Patternott, Coomaraswamy and at the very end Edwards.

Received from S Skandakumar via email on July 3 2010
At Madanghawatte Lane were the NAMASIVAYAMS, who
owned CEYLON PICTORIALS...the equivalent then of Nine
Hearts, Uthum Pathum of now, and their elder son
Rabindran was at Royal and went to the Campus with me.
In fact I used to cycle to and from his home for night joint
studies that helped me to clear the GSQ hurdle at the
University of Colombo...! Rabi married an English girl and
died in the UK a couple of years ago. His only sister,
Lohini, married Dr Sanath Nallainathan of Castle Lane
fame and they are settled in the US.

- S. Skandakumar

A Brothers Appreciation - by Kumaraswamy Velupillai –
Italy

Sockanathan - A Brother's Appreciation

My dear Daughters, Sister, Brothers, Cousins and Friends,

I copy below a feeble attempt at an 'appreciation' of my
elder brother. It is hard to disentangle emotions from
memories of innocent and honest splendour.
But I have given it a try.

Please feel free to pass it on to other cousins, friends and
whoever you think might want to remember Sockananthan
with fondness and gentleness.

Affectionately, Vela

Sockanathan – A Brother's Appreciation

It was the great Rabindranath Tagore who wrote:

'Peace, my heart, let the time for the parting be sweet.

Let it not be a death but completeness.'

These are lines that I have had to remember very often in recent years, as friends, contemporaries and relations have begun to bid sad farewell.

I had grown very fond of Sockanathan in recent years and we had developed, without intentions on either side, a pleasurable routine of ringing each other almost every Sunday, wherever I was. He was as always - and as far as my remembrances go, back on time's treacherous arrow - cheerful, light-hearted in touch, generous and humorous, none of the attributes I was ever able to cultivate. He seemed to have been endowed with these noble qualities, almost from birth.

In childhood, we had a different Sunday routine; after Sunday morning classes at the Ramakrishna Mission, we were given permission to walk on to my Paternal Aunt's home, down Ratnakara Place, for a sumptuous lunch. Rasathi Mami – my Aunt - would prepare a wonderful chicken curry - using that inherited talent from Paatti, my Grandmother - and shower us with food and sweets and love and kindness. Even though we were young boys, always wanting to be on the street down Madangahawatte Lane, playing cricket, we would never miss those enticing Sunday Lunches at Ratnakara Place. It came to an end in April, 1956, when we - alas - moved from 17 Madangahawatte Lane.

It may well be apposite to mention here that the unfortunate 1964 Royal College cricket team that lost to the Thomians contained four players who were born and lived, as neighbours, down Madangahawatte Lane, in the early 1950s: Sockanathan, Cedric Fernando, Lakshman Thalayasingham and Asoka Samarajeeva! I still recall, with pure pleasure, the cricket we played in the small Thalayasingham garden, in those halcyon days.

He was also, always, immensely more talented than I was, or even than any of my other siblings; anything he touched, in childhood, turned into success. I recall the grinding paths I had to carve for myself, for any meagre success I ever achieved when growing up. Large doses of luck and hard work were necessary ingredients in my path in life, and even then success was always tempered by failures. His talents, gifts and light-heartedness seemed almost to have been the 'winner's curse' - since he did not have to try too hard, he - perhaps - did not have to cultivate the disciplines one needs for survival in a world that is infested with the Red Queen syndrome.

When Sockanathan was a student at Madras Christian College, I think he once told me that he played and opened batting for the South Zone Universities the same year that Sunil Gavaskar opened for the West Zone Universities and they played against each other. This was, I think, in 1967. I visited Madras to see him, on my way from Kyoto to Colombo. I had booked a large room at the old Woodlands Hotel; Sockanathan, Rajan Namasivayam and Ramanan, Mr Ratnathickam, our shcool history teacher's nephew, came to meet me at Meenambakkam airport. We shared that one room I had booked and enjoyed three days of pure splendour - eating every night at the Madras Buhari Hotel.

My father once wrote me: 'Sockanathan is like an elephant; he does not know his own strengths'. I still have that letter Appa wrote me, in 1973.

It was wholly characteristic of him and wonderfully amusing when I last met him, at my Sister's daughter's wedding, to look hard at me, with unblinking eyes - in response to my embraced greeting - and ask me: 'And who are you?'. I nearly dropped with laughter, thinking he was, as usual, being that little bit mischievous!

I shared many moments of splendour with him, some even enchantingly comic.

When he first arrived in Sweden, he sat next to Shivantha Tambiyaiya, on the plane journey. During that journey he had shown his disfigured passport to Shivantha - disfigured by an unnecessary stamp by the British High Commission in Colombo; Shivantha, being slightly irresponsible, had taken it and scratched over the British High Commission stamp and told Sockanathan that 'they - the British High Commission - had no business stamping with seals that were not requested'!!!!

So, he arrived in Sweden, and with admirable and princely unconcern, showed me Shivantha's silly handiwork.

I was aghast and had to devise a most devious and totally improper way of dealing with it so that he could get his visa to go on to England. It was a method a Swiss Pastor in Chur in Switzerland had taught me, having practised it during his years as a Partisan in Ticino, near the Italian border, to help Italian Jews to escape across the border near Porlezza.

But Sockanathan was completely unfazed - either by Shivantha's totally callous act or by my own trepidations!!

That was typical of him.

Whenever we spoke, on our regular Sunday conversations, it was invariably also about cricket and whatever match was then going on. He kept himself fully informed of the current cricket scene.

Since about his last birthday I had begun sending him some of my older cricket books - by Cardus, Arlott, Ray Robinson and so on; they gave him great and undiluted pleasure, to read and reminisce. He remembered more than I could, about the times of Hassett and Morris, Laker and Lock, Lindwall and Miller, Ramadhin and Valentine. It was with tremendous enthusiasm that he would, time and time again, recite that great calypso about 'cricket lovely cricket ... with those two little friends of mine, Ramadhin and Valentine', celebrating that famous Lords victory by a West Indian side blessed with the legendary 3 Ws and Ramadhin and Valentine.

Like my Father, Sockanathan never had a cruel or unkind word or opinion of anyone or anything. He was wholly devoid of envy and completely innocent of greed.

We had been brought up in a relatively enlightened Hindu home, observing – as most Tamil Hindus of old Ceylon did – the usual rituals and ceremonies. However, at some point in the mid-1970s, Sockanathan, I think, felt the need for a more individually satisfying faith and embraced, wholeheartedly, the Christian faith. I rarely spoke to him about his commitment to his new found faith, nor the kind of sustenance the new beliefs gave him – partly because my own experiences of being a student at Kyoto, Lund and Cambridge during the turbulent late 1960s and early 1970s had radicalised my views and visions of Church and State. But I know, from his silences and serenities, that he was at peace with himself, in spite of personal difficulties during the last decade of his life.

My fond memories of childhood holidays, shared with Sockanathan and my elder Thiruchittampalam cousins – Rohini, Chandran and Sarojini - in innocence and honesty that only children can muster, are still a source of great happiness. We spent happy times in Chavakachcheri, Kankesanthurai, Kalkudah, Kalmunai, Bandarawela, Nuwara Eliya and Kurunegala. The memories of unadulterated enjoyments at Paasi Kudah are unforgettable. Another holiday, together with intimate class mates – Rajan Namasivayam, Ravi Somasundaram and Rabindran Namasivayam (our cousin), at an 'uncountry' Tea Plantation that was being managed by Rajan's maternal uncle (for S.J.V. Chelvanayagam) was one of our most cherished shared memory.

Now, alas, Sarojini, Sockanathan and Rabindran are not among us.

In Chavakachcheri, it was he who introduced me to the wonderful sands and taught me to appreciate the 'Manal Pitti', off the Jaffna Lagoon – these are, in fact my own earliest memories, going back to 1951 and 1952. Often, during the 'December holidays' spent in Chavakachcheri, we would be taken to Keerimalai, to bath in the holy waters and, then, after a wonderful breakfast of hot thosai or puttu, to the Kandasamy Temple in Nallur. Occasionally, after that, a visit to Sangili Thoopu, in Nallur, my Paternal Uncle's home, situated where – allegedly – Sangilian had his courtyard during his reign.

Sockanathan's own earliest personal sadness was experienced when he lost his close and much loved friend, Ronnie Fernando, who died under tragic circumstances. For years he kept a framed photograph of Ronnie in his room at home.

But I think – and feel – that he had come to terms with 'loss as a way of life', in a graceful and serene way. Perhaps it was his commitment to the faith he had embraced that gave him some inner strength to sustain and overcome grief and loss and tackle these imposters with a judicious combination of disdain and reluctant respect.

I would do him no justice if I did not mention the last few years at Royal College and the evenings and weekends spent playing cricket at 'Uncle's Paradise'!

The emotions and the enjoyments are impossible to describe in words – only those of us who were part of the 'Uncle's Paradise' community will know and understand what that camaraderie meant. The dusks, as the sun set, and as the last overs were being bowled, one began to savour the taste of the thosai or the rotti one was going to eat at Saraswathi Lodge or Buhari's or wherever one went, on any particular day, after a wonderful evening of cricket and friendship among friends. Often, the evening came to an end with more talk and gossip at the home of Norbert and Lloyd Perera, which was always open and welcomed all and sundry with immense kindness and generosity.

I will miss him and our routinised Sunday conversations - and for the inspiring light-heartedness that was infested with joy. But he has left me – and many others – with shared memories that enriched us in his lifetime and will enliven us in his absence, till we also reach him, and relive the past.

I can only recall Emily Dickinson's poignant words of Farewell, as dusk comes, yet again:

'Good-by to the life I used to live,And the world I used to know;And kiss the hills for me, just once;Now I am ready to go!'

Farewell to thee, my beloved and gentle Brother.

Vela

Hampden Lane

Between Madangahawatte and Arethusa were the twin-houses of the Vander Hoeven brothers - the one on the right was where Melba, Sonna and Christine lived with their father. I can't remember the names of the other Vander Hoeven family.

Next to them and at the very bottom of Arethusa Lane was the bare block of land where the Baas (who owned the kadé) tethered his cows. Later on, the youngest Jayamanne daughter (Dulcie) built a Montessori School on this land.

Baas' Kadé was the local café for the residents of the Alakandiya. I remember that my parents had a tab at the Kadé for their cigarettes. This was also the firewood depot for the neighbourhood. There were almost always disagreements about the actual weight and volume of the firewood as obviously wet timber was heavier than the dry. The house next to the kadé was where the Pollocks family lived and I remember the tock-tock of Joyce Pollocks' high-heel shoes as she walked up or down Arethusa Lane.

This is a tribute to the baby-boomers of the area – Heather Gallwey, Mohan Coomaraswamy and his siblings, Bala Kanagaratnam, Sonna & Christine Vander Hoeven, Cedric, Bryce & Christine Fernando, Christopher, Evans & Karyn Pereira, Honourine Abeykoon, Ranjit & Siri Jayatunga-Perera, David, Ranil, Michael & Sharmini Goonawardene, Ivan, Anne & Paul Martinus, late Harsha Abeywardene, Shirley-Joan Bartholomeusz and her siblings, Fran

Bartholomeusz, Janaka & Harsha Wijetunge, Janaka Rasiah, Kumar and Nedra Wagiswara, Rohan & Nilanthi Jayaratne, the Chuganis, Shantha & Chandra Wijeyrajah, Claude & Cheryl Wickeremasinghe, Suraj Perera and his siblings, Davanel & Radcliffe Flanderka, the Muhseens, Aloma Peiris, and the Sinnathamby girls............possibly many others whose names I can't remember, though I can picture their faces. I wonder where life has taken them?

Pereira Lane

The Anis (brother of Mohamed Sameer) family lived down this street.

Pennycuick Road

Pennyquick Road in Wellawatte is probably named for Charles Edward Ducat Pennycuick. Born in India in 1844, he lost his father Brigadier John Pennycuick at the Battle of Chillianwalla in the Punjab in 1849. He joined the Ceylon Civil Service and became Mayor of Colombo in 1893. Subsequently appointed Postmaster General, he finished his career as Treasurer of Ceylon, receiving a K.C.M.G. in retirement.

His elder brother, Colonel John Pennycuick, became quite famous in India. As an engineer in the Public Works Department, he built the Mullaiperiyar dam across the Periyar River in Kerala, and is worshipped as a god by farmers in the districts of the Madurai zone of Tamil Nadu, who irrigate their fields with waters from the reservoir.

On the other hand, C. E. D. Pennecuick's main claim to fame appears to be that, as Mayor, he considered objectionable the killing of stray dogs by drowning them in the Beira, so in 1894 he ordered the construction of a gas chamber for the purpose.

Vinod Moonesinghe - roar.lk - April 2018

37th Lane

Canal Lane

#5 Firoze Sameer

#7 the late Ansar

MCM Razeen

MIM Sahill

Zubair Rasheed

Basheer Ahamed

E S Fernando Mawatha (School Lane)

Kishore Lalvani

No 465 Galle Road, Wellawatte, Colombo 6

pic posted by Tharindu Amunugama on FB - Apr 9 2012

Sri Bodhirukkarama Mawatha (Vihara Lane)

Formerly known as Vihara Lane, this very narrow street where only one single vehicle could pass at a time, was later broadened to accommodate the massive traffic that plied between Galle Road and Sri Saranankara Road, that bordered the Wellawatte Canal, inland.

The massive Buddhist Temple located on the right side of the street gave rise to its new name of Sri Bodhirukkarama Mawatha. Most homes down this street were owned and occupied by the Buddhist Fernando families who later sold out to other communities.

During its hey days the street was notorious for its gang warfare and crime which was a regular scenario within its domain. The street widening project reduced the crime rate although the gangs still continued to roam its locality.

Some of the residents who lived down this street were the Malay family at the top left, Arasu's, Fernando's at No 19, Mrs Ibrahim and her children at No 21 who moved in from their previous abode at St. Peter's Place in Wellawatte.

46th Lane

Williams Avenue

Quarry Road

Rajaguru Sri Subuthi Road

Comments:
Anonymous

Great pictures. It's hard to believe that I lived in such a place. I was there in Hampden lane in 1981.

The pictures capture the day to day life of Sri Lankans- not sure if I can live there again.

Thanks for sharing.

10:46 AM, October 23, 2005

Anonymous

Hi

I used to live in 55th lane from 72-88, good to see the photos, very nostologic & bring back a lot of memories.

Thanks

11:42 AM, March 13, 2006

Anonymous

Nice Old pics- Great website- Keep it up

12:14 AM, April 11, 2006

Human Observer

Great stuff my man...i used to live in fussels lane
and the pictures just took me back.
I live in another country now but can never
forget the life in lanka.
cheers

6:20 AM, April 21, 2006

Human Observer

I lived in fussels lane from 88 to 2000 and it was
a golden time though i am not sure how it would
feel now,but,homes home.Nice job my man with
the pictures.keep updating with stories,cheers
mate,
SPC.FXF[marine corps]AZ

6:23 AM, April 21, 2006

Human Observer

great stuff man,,i used to live in fussels lane,i am
abroad now,.keep updating please,would like to
see some new stuff as the country and the whole
developing world is changing.I miss my life
their,cant go back though.

SPC,FXF [mc]AZ 1st infantry,3rd batalion.

6:27 AM, April 21, 2006

Anonymous

What a great webpage. It gives me more of an insight into the home place of my family's sponsored kids, my Australian/Sri Lankan friends (one of whose relatives crack a mention) and my favourite holiday destination.

Good job! Thanks.

8:14 PM, May 07, 2006

Anonymous

What a great trip down memory lane. I lived in Wellawatte till 1975 and then moved to Pamankade, but continued to do my marketting at Wella.One of the great residents of Wellawatte would be Elmer de Haan - he used to ride around on his bicycle with a monkey on the handlebars.

4:41 PM, July 27, 2006

Anonymous

I was recently in Colombo and visited Wellawatte. The sign post for Pereira Lane now reads "Pareira Lane" - an insult to the original residents of Pereira Lane, the parents of late Professor EOE Pereira. My late mother who grew up in Wellawatte in the mid-1900's used to tell us how they would wander through the Madan forest (now Madangahawatte Lane) to visit the Pereira children who went to St Clares College with my mother and her sister.

4:58 AM, July 28, 2006

Anonymous

Would love to see an old photo of Gordon Gardens. I remember so well as a kid - the huge statue of Queen Victoria and sitting under a tree filled with fruit bats. Also if anyone has an old photo of the miniature lighthouse that was torn down to build the Hilton, I think - it was at the very end of the Galle Face Green.

7:40 PM, October 16, 2006

Anonymous

This comment has been removed by a blog administrator.

2:40 PM, December 31, 2006

Anonymous

I remember Uncle Elmer. He was a great friend of my fathers. We used to visit his house down sinsapa road quite often. He used to play us classical records and comment on what was going on. I remember he gave me a record of 'Peter and the wolf', which I still have and treasure.

8:26 PM, January 05, 2007

Anonymous

My uncle, Launcelot de Soysa lived on
Racecourse Avenue, Colombo in the 60's with
his wife Marguerite De Soysa.
Did anyone know of him?
Thanks,
Sue
1:39 AM, November 07, 2007

Anonymous

Used to live at Frances road from 89 till 2002!
love it man! ur website brought back my school
days(alexandr college), days I used to spend at
the wellawatte beach with my friends.... those are
days that'll never come back in my life again!
love srilanka! especially wellawatte! recent visit
was on 2008(for a months time) still looks the
same! lots of vehicles though....! but I had the
hardest time coming back to Canada! LOVE U
SRILANKA N WILL MISS U FOREVER! it's a
void which no other country can fulfill....!
anyway! thx for this website man! great job.....!
keep it up! if u cud plz update with some latest
pics.!

5:35 AM, March 13, 2008 🗑

caroline

Your article was really interesting - especially for someone who is trying to trace their heritage. I live and was born in London in 1960. My grandfather was called Vincent Mendis Abeysekera (changed to Abeysakera in England) and was definitely in London from 1912 onwards - probably earlier. He was the son of Matilda Abeysekera (nee de Abrew) who died aged 79 on April 11 at the home of her son Absolom on Siriwickerema Road, Wellawatte (I don't know what year). Her husband was W C M Abeysekera, her sisters Mrs Elen Karunaratne, Mrs Alice Karunaratne and Mrs Harriet de Zoysa. Her brother was P R de Abrew. She had two granddaughters called Ina and Brenda Abeysekera - I believe one of them married to become a de Silva. My mother was Vanda Grace Chase (nee Abeysakera) and her mother was Naomi Lucy (a white European and the second wife of Vincent). Please, can anyone help me trace this family?

<u>12:07 PM, July 15, 2008</u>

Anonymous
HI,

Do you know the name of the theatre (now demolished) that used to be opposite the Savoy Wellawatta close to the canal?

<u>11:27 AM, September 14, 2009</u>

Faz

Yes, it was called The Plaza Cinema and used to show Tamil Movies from South India featuring such heroes as MGR, Shivaji Ganeshan, Gemini Ganeshan, Nambiar, Veerappa etc.

<u>11:42 AM, September 14, 2009</u>

Thaku

It was fun going down memory lane Arethusa Lane, I felt for a moment that I was there right now. What fun we had can never forget the good times and lovely memories.

<u>7:22 PM, July 02, 2010</u>

Sherin Vasukhi Emmanuel (nee Alexander)
We the Alexanders lived at 27 Madangahawatte Road from the early 1960's to late 1970's. Mr & Mrs Alexander and their 7 children and families live in Ontario Canada. Mr Alexander passed away in My 2009 at age 83. We have many memories of our life on Madangawatte lane and continue to be in contact with the Patternotts (#33) in Australia and USA, The Coomaraswamys in Australia, UK and Canada, The Selvarajah's in USA and SriLanka, The Namiasivayam's in USA and UK plus many of our then neighbours.

Faz

Thanks for the update on Madangahawatte Lane, Sherin. We used to be scared to cycle down that street since it was so narrow. We used Hampden Lane and 37th Lane.

12:14 AM, October 21, 2010

Geoff Ells

Thanks! Fantastic insights into Colombo life and a great source of interesting facts.
I'm writing a book on the origin of the street names of Colombo and you've given me quite a few answers and clues.
Do you know where the name Fussel comes from? This is one puzzle I'd love to solve...
G E O F F

8:23 AM, August 17, 2011

Faz

your welcome Geoff. No clue abt the origins of "Fussel's Lane". It must be an Englishman I bet?

2:18 PM, August 17, 2011

Anonymous

Wonderful post.. Thank you very much.

I lived down Arethusa Lane from 1973 onwards, my mother still lives there and so do many of the longer-term residents, (No 6, 8, 10x) Goonetilleke's, De La Zilwas, Wickremasinghes .. Britto and De Silva at 38 and 40 respectively and more
SD

9:58 PM, February 22, 2012

Anonymous

hey d alexendra pic is my father man

10:58 AM, April 08, 2012

Anonymous Hi

i realise this post is 8 years old.

quote

Between Madangahawatte and Arethusa were the twin-houses of the Vander Hoeven brothers - the one on the right was where Melba, Sonna and Christine lived with their father. I can't remember the names of the other Vander Hoeven family

unquote

I think i am a decendant of the above van der Hoeven family. Is it possible that the brothers went by the names Charles and George (george being my grandfather) They left for Australia in 1948...

cheers
Nicholas van der Hoeven

8:32 AM, March 01, 2013

Faz

received from Jen in Australia:
Hi Faz

I don't know the names of the 2 older gentlemen who owned these two houses; but I do know that the son of one of them (if I remember his name was Brian) migrated to Australia around the 1950s; a son of the other gentlemen went to live in Germany.

Sonna (Melville was his real name) was killed in an accident on the Galle Road, Wellawatte in 2011.

Jenny

10:06 AM, March 01, 2013

Anonymous
Hi, I live down Dhammarama Road number 60.
I am still there. Number 58 next house is where Asanga Gurusinghe srilankan cricket was staying. Wellawatte produced very good athletes , sportsman. Dinali De Silva, who had four Sri lankan records and the greatest athlete Visakha Vidhyalaya produced was my sister.

The first Sri Lanka ever to get World Boxing Refree tittle by qualification was my father Thomas de Silva, who officiated at seven consecutive Asian Games and one World Championships.

Then there was Asantha De Mel, Sri Lanka pace bowler and chief selector, Sujan Subramaniam Sri Lankan Rugby Captain, his brother Sukku, thambipillais brothers, Theodore, David and Christo all Thomians.Christo is present CF n FC president.
Cricketers, Priyal, Gihan de Silva who played for STC. Deepal Dalpathadu, who played fro Royal and managed the Peterson Sports Club for so many years.there were all from Peterson Lane.

    5:11 AM, April 08, 2013 🗑

Lali

    Hi, I lived down Alexandra Terrace in the 80's. Thanks for the update of Alexandra Road. What fun we had can never forget the good times and lovely memories.
    Lali from UK

3:48 PM, April 09, 2013

Anonymous

    Great work, bringing back sweet memories of Wella, and specially, Alexandra road which was my home from a tiny tot until I moved to Australia in 1987....

Studied in HFC Bamba, lived opposite to Annasamy's house. Lali should remember me... Did Accountancy with Dinali DeSilva from Dhammarama Road, who has her EARLY morning run in the beach and comes straight to my place to put me up from sleep to do some combine studies before exams.... GOOD OLD DAYS, will never come back...

7:41 AM, April 12, 2013

Anonymous

Great work on Wella, bringing back sweet memories, specially of Alexandra Road which was my home from a tiny tot to 1987 when I moved to Australia. Studied at HFC Bamba, lived across Annasamy's. Lali should remember me. Studied Accountancy with Dinali of Dhammarama Road. Will cherish memories forever...

7:49 AM, April 12, 2013

<u>Faz</u>

Hi Lali, you must surely remember Ramani, Babujee, Sada, Shankaran & Co at old man Annasamy's Place?

Sadly they had to pack up and leave after 1983
when their factory, General Metals at Kelaniya
was burned down. Sada is in Tamil Nadu while
Babujee has passed away. They were very close
to our family even though we lived in Bamba
and we sued to play Bridge every weekend at
their place. Bless them all. Beautiful people!

11:06 AM, April 12, 2013

Lali

Hi Fazli

Yes, I knew Ramani well, Babujee and Sada
were my brothers good friends. Sorry to hear
about Babujee. I really miss Alexandra Road, all
the good times I had. Your article has brought
back many memories, thank you for writing it.

Lali

7:59 PM, April 16, 2013

Lali

Yes, of course I remember you, how can I forget
the good times we had. I used to love the every
morning run with Dinai, it kept us fit! I too agree
the good old days will never come back, but gald
we had them.

Lali

8:53 PM, April 16, 2013

Faz

I am still in touch with Sada through his daughter Sachu in Chennai. Cant forget the old days we had together since the 60s

8:56 PM, April 16, 2013 🗑

Anonymous

Hi Wonderful to go back in time, i left colombo in 1972, trying to locate a friend Kamala Thomas who was staying at 17, 41st lane ,would be great to reconnect my present no
is +27743837175,email panchoscn@yahoo.com thanks - Shashi

8:04 PM, December 15, 2013

Unknown

Hi
I need help.
Can anybody give info about THE COLOMBO STUDIO OF 1940/50s at kumarakom ratnapura road ??
It was owned/operated by one mr krishnan nair whose wife was rajalakshmi .
He owned studio in trico mallee also and hotel ananda
Bhavan
What happened . Where are they.
Any clues .?

9:40 PM, September 16, 2015

Anonymous

I used to live in 32nd lane from 1940 till I married in 1958. My mother and stepfather continued living there, in the same house till they migrated to Australia in 1973. Most of the residents in 32nd Lane were either Burgher or Tamil. Very few Sinhalese families lived there while I was there.

<u>3:33 AM, November 03, 2015</u>

Anonymous

Bryce Fernando, lives in Geneva, Switzerland wife's name is Aysha and has 2 children both married and grandfather of 2. His sister Christine died recently, was married with one daughter and lived in Dehiwela with her husband and daughter down Roberts road until the time of her death

<u>6:59 PM, November 03, 2015</u>

George

If you lived in 32nd Lane you would have known the VanTwests. Theirs was the first house on the right. Mr VanTwest was superintendent of the Govt Publications Bureau.

All his sons were at Royal. Good cricketers, boxers and athletes. One of the boys Errol, was with me at Royal Prep and Thurstan. They also moved to Australia and settled in Queensland. Errol worked at the Commonweath Bank until he passed away a few years ago.

George Rupesinghe
Sydney Australia

8:21 AM, November 08, 2015

Unknown

Nice to see my grand father Carl Thiedeman been mentioned. His wife was Daphne and their children the late Ralston and Beverley who married Mervyn Dirckze of 8 Lorensz Road Bambalapitiya. I am their daughter. Mervyn's mother worked at Savoy Cinema selling tickets and his father Errol Dirckze a WWII veteran worked at Arcadia shoe shop in Colombo 3.

8:37 PM, July 05, 2016

About the Compiler

Fazli Sameer was born, on 16 February, 1948, in Bambalapitiya, Colombo-4, and was educated in the English Medium at Royal Primary School (1953-58) and Royal College (1959-66), Colombo. In 1967/68 he spent the first year of the course in BSc. Physical Science at the University of Colombo and left thereafter to pursue a course in Computer Science with IBM.

His employment covered stints at Chartered Bank in Colombo (1979-89), Citibank in the Middle East (1979-1999), Al Faisaliah Group in Saudi Arabia (1999-2008) in Information Technology, and private Business & IT Consulting from 2008 to date.

Since 1979, Fazli has been engaged in researching, collecting, and publishing genealogy data of all Sri Lankan communities. He published, Family Tree Data: Genealogical Tables of Sri Lankan Muslims in 1996, and manages the Sri Lanka Genealogy Website on the internet at the link:

http://www.worldgenweb.org/lkawgw

Fazli has also been researching, preserving and publishing the history and legacy of Sri Lankan people, places, and significant events. He writes and manages a blog, titled F's Place which contains valuable data of streets, people, homes, and families who lived in Colombo in the 1960s: http://kermeey.blogspot.com

He is also into prose and poetry on his personal blog. F's Space: http://kermeey2.blogspot.com

He has been contributing to the English Writers Workshop, previously held at the Beach Wadiya, in Wellawatte, since January 2019.

Fazli married Shirani Ibrahim in 1974. They have two daughters, Melina & Nadia and two grandkids, Maria & Abdullah.

Reading and writing was always a great passion in the Sameer household in Bambalapitiya, in Colombo. Newspapers, magazines, and books were freely available, in abundance, for everyone to indulge in. The bookman, who rode all his novels on the back of a bike, was a regular visitor to the home.

Fazli is also the author of "Bamba Days" published in Aug 2020 which describes the people, streets, homes, families and events in the town of Bambalapitiya (Colombo 00400) in the 60s. He also published a collection of poetry titled "February Frolic" in 2020 and a collection of 13 volumes of Sri Lankan Muslim Family Genealogy in 2021. Sophie Akka & Somapala, Autobiography, Islamic Inheritance Q&A are also some of his works.

ooOoo

There are too many people who have contributed their memories to make this collection of "Wellawatte Ways" real, and, it will be impossible to name them all in order to convey my appreciation for their valuable efforts.

One positive outcome of this exercise has been the exuberance of the true nature of family that prevailed within the hearts and minds of the people who lived in the town of Wellawatte, in Colombo, in the 60s.

"Mother do you think they'll drop the bomb?"

[Pink Floyd – The Wall Album]

www.ingramcontent.com/pod-product-compliance
Lightning Source LLC
Chambersburg PA
CBHW050032260726
48658CB00005B/1564